Netaji Subhas Chandra Bose

Netaji Subhas Chandra Bose was born on 23rd January 1897, in Cuttack, in a famous family. His father was Janakinath Bose, reputed advocate. His mother was Prabhavati Devi, who was a cultured and learned lady. She had full faith in Ramakrishna Paramhansa. His family originally hailed from Bengal.

At that time, entire India was passing through tribulations. Bengal was the first province of India that was taken over by British.

At the age of five, he was admitted in the Baptist Mission School. Lady teachers were more in numbers here than the male teachers. Syllabus of the school was structured in such a way so that Indian children would be detached from the indigenous culture and thoughts and must adapt themselves to the western thoughts.

Since childhood, Subhas had a deep inclination towards studies. Because of his interest in his studies, his school teachers started adoring him very much. His manners had changed in such a way that it did not appear that he is an Indian. He had developed such a strong liking for the use of English words and English manners that even Anglo-Indian students were far behind him. Hep was fond of wearing a neat dress. He was highly alert and arrogant. His behaviour and manner was very much refined.

At the age of 12, he was admitted into the Roweshaw Collegiate School. This school gave much importance to Indian culture, language and education methods. The Principal of that school,

Beni Prasad Madhav, was imbued with nationalistic feelings. He revolted against the British Government and used to dream of an independent India. For this, he was engaged in preparing such an environment that he should be prepared for the struggle against India. He used to sit among children and used to teach him to love own country and culture.

Gradually, in the mind of child Subhas, there developed a strong hatred towards the Britishers. He was deeply affected by the association, religious thoughts and love towards the country. Subhas became much more interested towards knowing the culture of the country. He used to question him, and Madhav used to listen attentively to all his queries and then answer his queries. Subhas was so much influenced by the simple lifestyle of his ancestors and sages that he himself tried to follow those ideals in his life.

He always thought about his society and people whole-heartedly. An incident of his childhood gives evidence of his kind nature. When Subhas used to sit to eat, then he used to keep apart two chappatis from his dinner. Once when mother happened to look at the almirah, she was perplexed. A long line of ants was proceeding towards the almirah; after opening, she found out two chappatis in its corner. When mother asked Subhas about it, he replied in a grave manner. "You throw out these chappatis, there is no need of it now."

But his mother asked its reason reluctantly. Then Subhas said, "There lived an old beggar woman near our school. There was none in the world to look after her. I used to take daily these chappatis for her, but yesterday she expired, so, these chappatis are no more needed. Hearing this, mother became overwhelmed

with affection and embraced her son.

Gradually, the feelings of patriotism began to influence his mind. He was fearless, but after sometime, this fearlessness was reflected in his speech too. On 11 August, 1910, it was the first anniversary of the famous martyr Khudiram Bose. Just one year ago, because of his involvement in revolutionary activities, the British regime had sentenced him to death. On that day, Subhas assembled all the students of his school and gave a very good lecture on Khudiram Bose. In the school campus, a mourning ceremony was organised. All the students and teachers offered their obituary to him.

All friends of Subhas were so much influenced by him that they all used to assemble at his mere suggestion. He used to carry out each and every responsibility assigned to him. Subhas used to love his classmates very much and was very much concerned with their well-being.

Once there was an outbreak of cholera in a nearby village. Subhas and his friends were wholeheartedly engaged in the service of the sufferers. They used to visit each home, to serve the poor and ill-stricken, and used to arrange medicines for them. He himself took every initiative in cleanliness works. At this attempt, villagers were very much impressed.

During those days, Subhas was under much mental pressure. He was so much pained by the sufferings and pain of others that he used to remain restless. By chance, one day, he found a book written by Swami Vivekananda. Thoughts of Swamiji had a deep impact on his heart. Restlessness to free the country from poverty and ignorance and acquire political independence, was seen in the reflections of Swami Vivekanada.

In the year 1915, Subhas passed his intermediate exams, but he could not get good marks. Thereafter he started preparing for B.A. examination.

Once an English teacher of the college beat him severely. At this, Subhas became very much angry. His feeling of self-pride was aroused. He decided to avenge this insult.

After college hours, Subhas and his friends hid themselves near the college gate. As soon as the teacher came out of the college, everybody came upon him and beat him mercilessly. Next day, Subhas was turned out of the college. When Janakinath Bose, father of Subhas, came to know about it, he became very much worried about the future of his son, even then, he respected his feelings.

In July 1917, due to the attempts by the vice-chancellor Sri Ashutosh, Subhas was admitted in the B.A. three-year degree course. In this, besides other subjects, military training too was imparted. In the heart of Subhas, an interest for military exercise developed and he also was admitted there.

At the age of twenty, Subhas passed his BA examination. He stood second among all the successful students in Calcutta university. After this, his father advised him to prepare for the civil services examination.

At heart, the desire to work for the independence of the country was aroused, so he wanted to serve his country while living in the country. He put this proposal before his father. His father expressed with displeasure that to qualify for the civil services exam is difficult. “I know that you are avoiding this exam because you are afraid that you may not be able to pass the exams”. These words of his father had a deep impact upon him and he soon decided to prepare

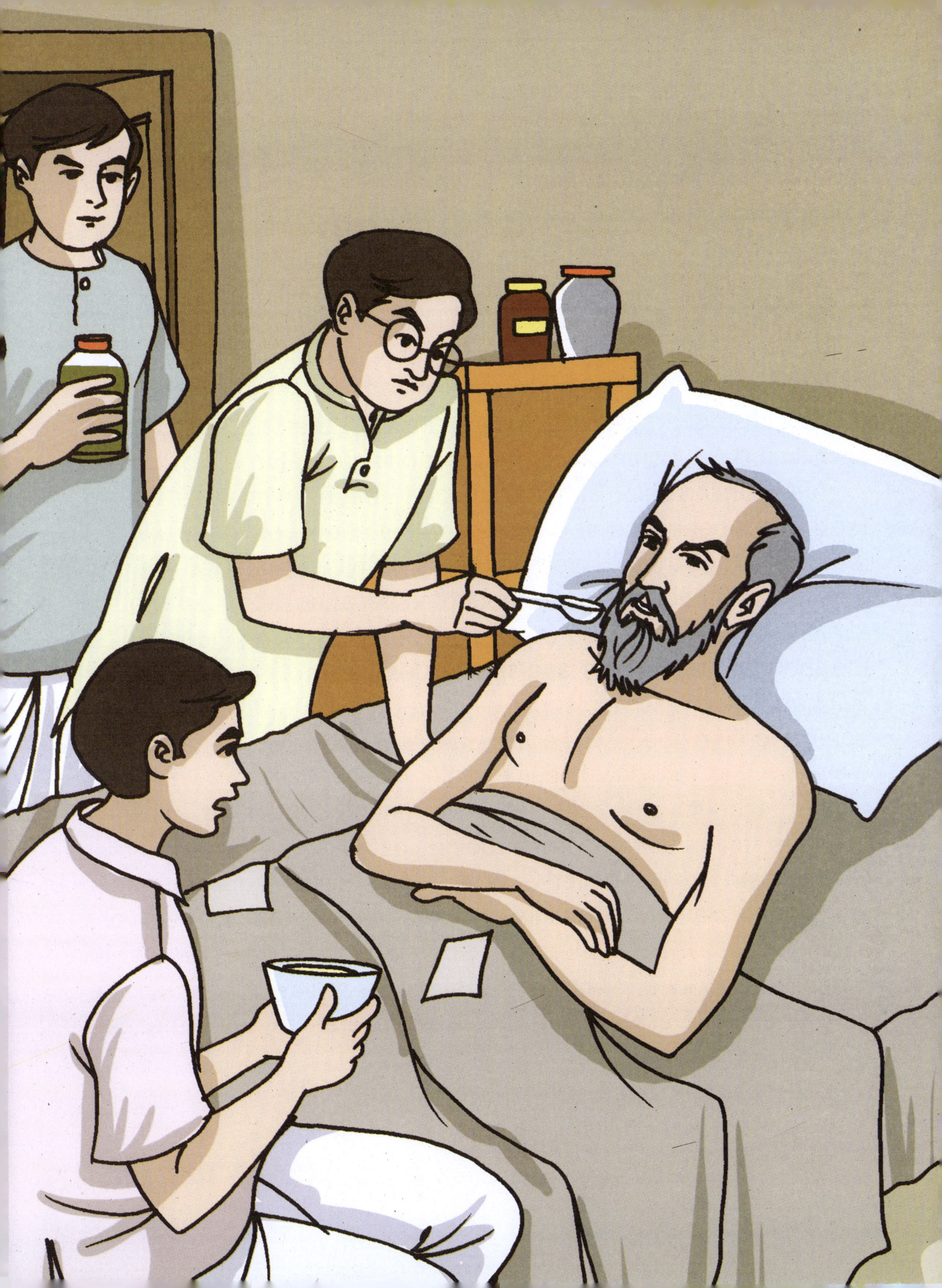

himself to go to London. After reaching London, Subhas sought admission in Cambridge University and started preparing hard for the exams. When the results for the civil services exams were declared, Subhas turned out to be successful.

By successfully passing in the civil services exams, he proved that Indian youths were in no way less capable than the British.

Subhas, too, was satisfied that he had honoured the name of his father in society. At the same time, he also proved his faith. But he did not want to lead a comfortable life by being a faithful officer of the British regime which enslaved India. Therefore, he resigned from the I.C.S. (Indian Civil Services) and again returned to India.

After coming back, Subhas met many leaders who were fighting for the independence of the country. He attentively heard all the leaders. During those days, he met Babu Chittaranjan Das. He was very much affected by his thoughts, because both nurtured a similar view. Chittaranjan Das, too, was very much influenced by the thoughts of Subhas and his wisdom. Then, he decided that Subhas would also accompany him. At that time, the movement against foreign goods was at its peak. At various places, the people were burning foreign goods. People were vacating government offices, schools and colleges. Throughout the nation, national colleges for students were being established. Deshbandhu Chittaranjan Das appointed Subhas as the principal of the college, known as National College. He found this opportunity very advantageous. Thereafter, he started sowing the seeds of discipline and love for one's motherland. On the other hand, he accompanied Deshbandhu Chittaranjan Das in a full-fledged manner to the cause of service to the nation.

On the other hand, he was engaged in the independence

struggle with Deshbandhu.

In 1921, in Baigawada, amidst the session of Indian National Congress, Subhas was appointed as the chief of the volunteer army. He was arrested on December 6 by British army and was imprisoned for six months. This was the first prison tour of Subhas.

While in prison, Subhas, rebuked a soldier employed on duty because he was not letting his secretary come inside. That soldier complained to the prison officer about Subhas. After that he was transferred to Berhampur jail. After staying there for some time, he was sent to Mandalay jail in Burma.

There were other prisoners too in Mandalay jail. Subhas had a psychological analysis of them. Political prisoners and bishops of Burma too, came in his contact. He had gathered important political information regarding the local politics of Burma, and the guerilla warfare over there. After being freed from the prison, he returned to his own country.

In 1922, Bengal was under the attack of a devastating flood. Hundreds of villages were washed away, thousands drowned in the midst of floods. In the moment of crisis, Subhas Babu devoted himself wholeheartedly to the service of the people. He also received the full co-operation of people. His leadership was appreciated everywhere.

In November 1926, the elections of regional legislative council in Bengal were held. At that time, he was in prison. He fought elections while in prison, and he was elected from Calcutta constituency.

After that, the health of Subhas Chandra Bose deteriorated further. He was taken to Rangoon for a medical check-up. From there, he was again taken to Calcutta. On the way, he was stopped

for inspection. After the inspection, when the investigation report was sent to the Governor-General, he was granted freedom.

After coming out of the prison, he found that the situation of the country was deteriorating rapidly. Swaraj party had lost its pride, everywhere Hindu-Muslim riots had erupted. In this situation, Gandhi too had kept himself aloof from politics and devoted himself wholeheartedly towards the upliftment of harijans. Subhas Chandra Bose too went to Sabarmati Ashram to meet Gandhi, but there was a difference in outlook between the two. Subhas had to return disappointed at that time. He was too much pained at this.

On the other hand, patriots like Ram Prasad Bismil, Jogesh Chatterjee, Shachindra Sanyal etc. were working under the leadership of Chandrashekhar Azad. It was their plan to establish *swaraj* by turning the Britishers out of the country.

On 3rd February, 1928, the Congress Executive Committee started movement throughout the country against the Simon Commission. The Police too adopted a rigid attitude. Everywhere *lathi*-charge took place, in which hundreds of people were wounded. On that occasion, Subhas Chandra Bose was leading the young generation.

Meanwhile, Subhas Chandra Bose travelled to different countries of Europe for four years. He was in search of other policies for the freedom of the country apart from the policy of Gandhiji.

Subhas Chandra Bose was unmarried. He was then 37 years old. He decided that he will again come upon the British government like a tiger and will defeat them and make the country forever free from the slavery of British.

He proceeded towards Britain on 8th January, 1938. In his

absence, he was appointed the President of Congress.

After being elected President, he returned to India. Few days after that incident, there started a wide divergence of opinion among Gandhi and Subhas. At the call of Gandhiji, most of the members resigned from the working committee. At this, Subhas Chandra Bose resigned from the post after being deeply hurt over that incident.

Subhas was a man of active nature. The spirit of freedom dominated his mind and body. Therefore, without wasting time, he organised one party of his own within the Congress Party which was known as 'Forward Bloc'. Inspite of the widespread differences between thought processes and work style, Subhas Babu had deep reverence and respect for Gandhiji. Even then, both of them could not associate together.

When in 1940, Subhas Chandra Bose started a movement to destroy Blackhole, a monument of the British. The British Government sent him to prison after arresting him. After that, the monument was destroyed, but Subhas was not freed. Therefore he went on a hunger strike in the prison, but he was imprisoned and was put on high alert.

During his imprisonment, he made an excuse of loneliness. After that one day, he disguised himself as a Maulavi and befooled the guards and proceeded towards Kabul. There he met some leaders and ambassadors and then he went to Germany and from there he went to Japan. Subhas Chandra Bose himself took control of the 'Azad Hind Fauj', he founded in Japan.

On 5th July, 1943, in Singapore, Netaji announced for the independence of India in a crowded gathering. He gave this slogan–"You give me blood, I will give you independence."

This speech of Netaji inspired everyone in the meeting. Young men decided to take a vow to sacrifice everything in the struggle for independence. All the ladies handed over their ornaments to Subhas. All the members present there, signed on the declaration with their blood. In this struggle, all the ladies also participated with their male counterparts. Netaji, in his Azad Hind Fauj, admitted women in large numbers as soldiers. During the Second World War, Azad Hind Fauj defeated the British army so many times and started proceeding rapidly.

But when Japan surrendered and Germany too was defeated, then all the help given to Azad Hind Fauj was restricted and many of its army men were captured. People wanted to protect Subhas from being captured, so on 24th April, 1945, he was sent to Bangkok by a plane. From there, he went to Singapore, but unfortunately that aircraft met with a mishap. It is believed that, in that mishap Subhas Chandra Bose died.

Indian people have much reverence for Subhas, no one believed the news of his death in the mishap for many years.

His emphatic speech and his teachings are a source of inspiration for us even today.